SPOT-THE-DIFFERENCE MASTERPIECES | 40 EYE-BENDING FINE-ART PUZZLES

Find the
**800 ingenious
differences** in
this grown-up
activity book

SPOT-THE-DIFFERENCE
MASTERPIECES | 40 EYE-BENDING
FINE-ART PUZZLES

PUZZLE
WRIGHT
PRESS
New York

PUZZLE
WRIGHT
PRESS

New York

An Imprint of Sterling Publishing Co., Inc.
1166 Avenue of the Americas
New York, NY 10036

© 2016 Octopus Publishing Group
This Puzzlewright edition published in 2017.
Concept and images from The Art Archive Ltd.

ISBN 978-1-4549-2720-4

Distributed in Canada by Sterling Publishing Co., Inc.
c/o Canadian Manda Group, 664 Annette Street
Toronto, Ontario, Canada M6S 2C8

For information about custom editions, special sales,
and premium and corporate purchases, please contact
Sterling Special Sales at 800-805-5489 or
specialsales@sterlingpublishing.com.

Manufactured in China

www.sterlingpublishing.com
www.puzzlewright.com

CONTENTS

INTRODUCTION

Great works of art deserve a closer look. The 40 masterpieces featured in this book represent some of the highest achievements in European art, and their beauty is matched with a keen sense of detail throughout the frame. Indeed, sometimes the most interesting elements of a painting are tucked away – a subtle interaction between two characters in the background, or even a wry expression on someone's face. These exquisite elements all come together to make a painting greater than the sum of its parts, and are worth investigating scrupulously.

Toward that end, each of the following paintings has had 20 details subtly changed. The original is on the left page, and the altered version on the right. As you peruse each painting and spot each difference, you'll become intimately familiar with every square inch of these famous masterpieces, and rewarded with a deep understanding of what makes them so extraordinary.

A BAR AT THE FOLIES-BERGÈRES
Édouard Manet
1882
Courtauld Institute of Art Gallery, London
The Art Archive / DeA Picture Library

There's a spot-the-difference game to be played with the mirror image in this famous painting. Can you see what the painter has missed from the foreground?

Answers to the puzzles
are in the back of the book:
follow the grid references
to discover the changes

LA PRIMAVERA (SPRING) (DETAIL)

Giuseppe Arcimboldo
1563
Real Academia de Bellas Artes de San Fernando, Madrid
The Art Archive / Academia BB AA S Fernando / Gianni Dagli Orti

It is sometimes suggested that Arcimboldo's wildy imaginative paintings were the products of an unbalanced mind, but his Renaissance audience adored puzzles, symbolism and the bizarre. Arcimboldo's art went on to inspire the Surrealists many centuries later.

LAS MENINAS (FAMILY OF KING PHILIP IV OF SPAIN) (DETAIL)

Diego Velázquez
1656
Museo del Prado, Madrid
The Art Archive / Museo del Prado Madrid / Gianni Dagli Orti

This much-analyzed painting contains its own puzzle. Is it intended as a portrait of the five-year-old Infanta and her attendants? Or is Velázquez painting the King and Queen, whose reflection we see in the mirror in the background, standing where the viewer stands?

A B C D E F G H I J K L M N O P Q R S T U V W X Y Z
1 2 3 4 5 6 7 8 9 10 11 12 13 14 15 16 17 18 19 20 21 22 23 24 25 26

**CHRIST IN THE HOUSE
OF MARTHA AND MARY**

Pieter Aertsen
1553
Museum Boijmans Van Beuningen, Rotterdam
The Art Archive / DeA Picture Library

Within this abundant scene, notice the dress of the different groups of people; while the group on the left are wearing contemporary sixteenth-century clothing, the cluster on the right are wearing Biblical dress, like those in the painting-within-a-painting in the background.

THE PARROT CAGE

Jan Steen
1665
Rijksmuseum, Amsterdam
The Art Archive /
DeA Picture Library

Jan Steen's works often
include domestic details.
Here, we can see the woman
on the left cooking oysters on
the fire. Notice the skill with
which Steen renders the
fabric of the woman's skirt;
capturing textures was one
of the painter's specialities.

A B C D E F G H I J K L M N O P Q R S T U V W X Y Z

1 2 3 4 5 6 7 8 9 10 11 12 13 14 15 16 17 18 19 20 21 22 23 24 25 26

A B C D E F G H I J K L M N O P Q R S T U V W X Y Z

**THE COURTYARD OF
A HOUSE IN DELFT**

Pieter de Hooch
1658
National Gallery, London
*The Art Archive /
DeA Picture Library*

This harmonious painting
shows the painter's interest
in domestic architecture.
The engraved stone that we
see above the arch originated
from an ancient cloister and
still exists today in an old
wall in Delft.

A SUNDAY ON LA GRANDE JATTE

Georges Seurat
1884–1886
Art Institute of Chicago
The Art Archive / DeA Picture Library

In this well-known Pointillist painting, Seurat used a new color pigment, zinc yellow, to show bright highlights on the sunlit grass. These have since discolored; imagine just how striking the contrast between sunlight and shadow would originally have been.

AMOROUS COUPLE

Johannes Vermeer
c. 1657–1658
Frick Collection, New York
*The Art Archive / Frick Collection,
New York / Superstock*

This painting includes many characteristics
of Vermeer's work, perhaps most noticeably
the soft light coming in from the window
on the left, and the contrast between light
and shade. The painter may have used a
camera obscura to create the perspective
of the scene.

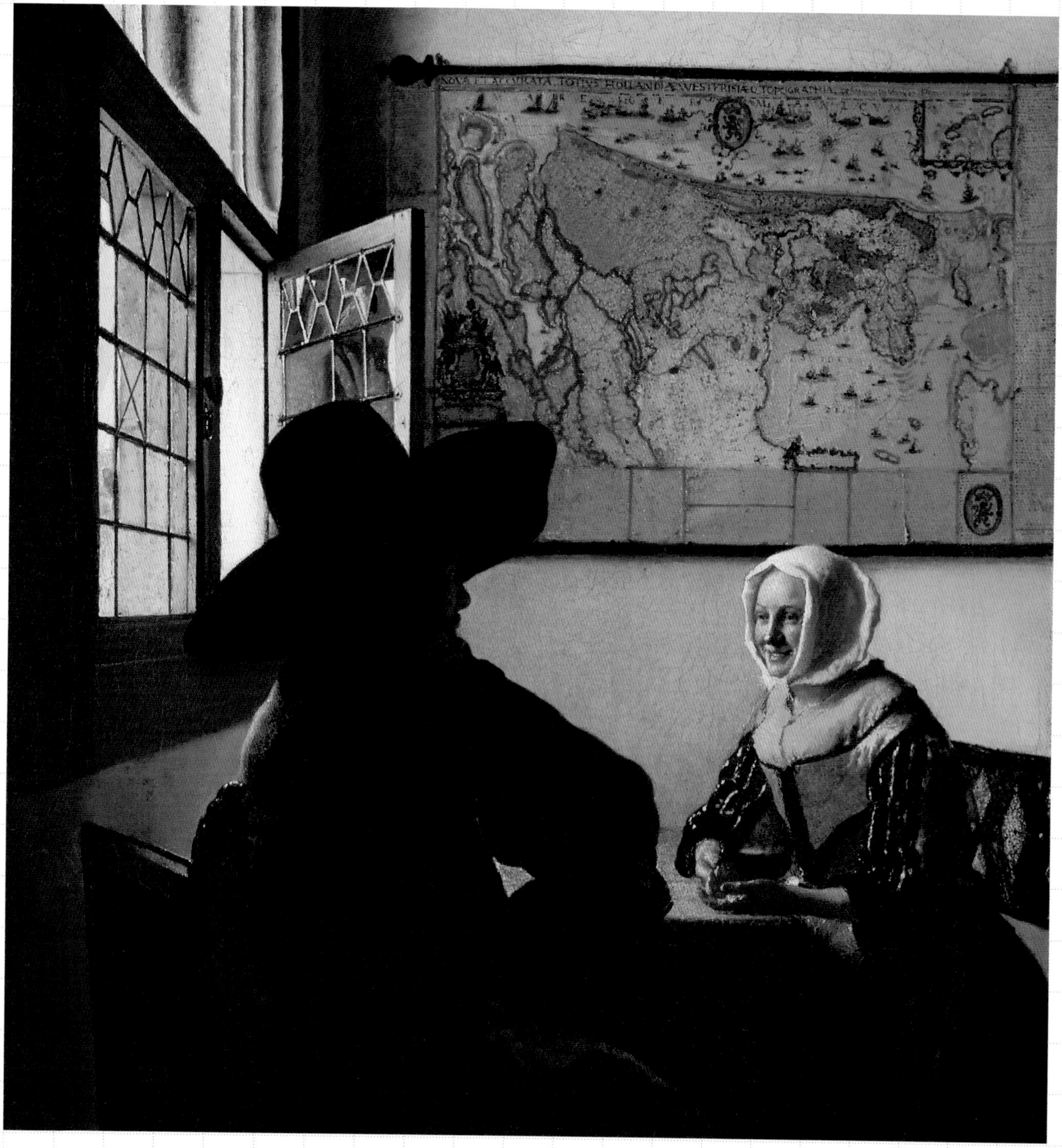

CHRIST PRESENTED
TO THE PEOPLE

Quentin Massys
1518–1520
Museo del Prado, Madrid
The Art Archive /
Museo del Prado Madrid

Massys was a skilled and serious
portrait painter but his depiction
of people sometimes borders on the
grotesque. Admire the rendering of
stone and marble on the cathedral
façade. Did you notice the double-
headed Habsburg eagle on the pennant?

A B C D E F G H I J K L M N O P Q R S T U V W X Y Z

1 2 3 4 5 6 7 8 9 10 11 12 13 14 15 16 17 18 19 20 21 22 23 24 25 26

A B C D E F G H I J K L M N O P Q R S T U V W X Y Z

**THE BELOVED
(THE BRIDE)**

Dante Gabriel Rossetti
1865–1866
Tate Gallery, London
*The Art Archive /
DeA Picture Library*

This famous Pre-Raphaelite
painting illustrates the Song
of Solomon; some words from it
are written on the frame. Notice
the bride's beautiful Peruvian
headdress and the rich and
ornate fabric from a Japanese
kimono that makes up her
bridal gown.

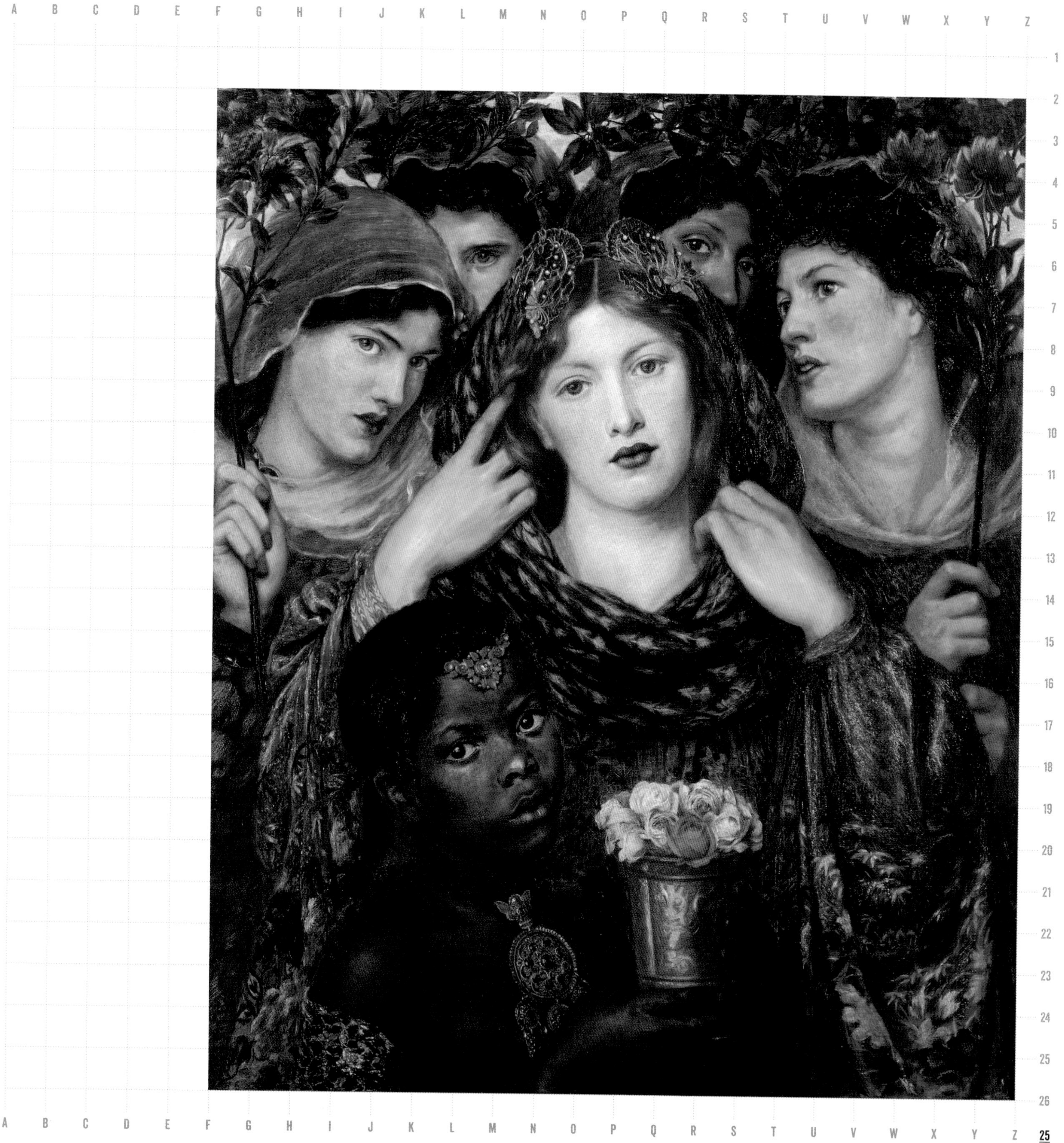
A B C D E F G H I J K L M N O P Q R S T U V W X Y Z
1 2 3 4 5 6 7 8 9 10 11 12 13 14 15 16 17 18 19 20 21 22 23 24 25 26

A B C D E F G H I J K L M N O P Q R S T U V W X Y Z

1 2 3 4 5 6 7 8 9 10 11 12 13 14 15 16 17 18 19 20 21 22 23 24 25 26

THE AMBASSADORS

Hans Holbein the Younger
1533
National Gallery, London
The Art Archive / DeA Picture Library

This fascinating painting, created the year Elizabeth I was born, contains a macabre visual puzzle. To see it properly, one must be either very high on the right or very low on the left; what is it?

A B C D E F G H I J K L M N O P Q R S T U V W X Y Z

A B C D E F G H I J K L M N O P Q R S T U V W X Y Z

1 2 3 4 5 6 7 8 9 10 11 12 13 14 15 16 17 18 19 20 21 22 23 24 25 26

A B C D E F G H I J K L M N O P Q R S T U V W X Y Z

**CABINET OF CURIOSITIES
(WITH GLASS DOORS)
WITH VARIOUS OBJECTS**

Andrea Domenico Remps
1621–1699
Opificio delle Pietre Dure, Florence
*The Art Archive / DeA Picture Library /
G. Nimatallah*

The painting is arranged so that
we appear to be looking straight
into the cabinet. But the mirror
affords us a tiny glimpse of the
room in which the cabinet was
painted; the broken panes of
glass make the cabinet look all
the more real.

A BAR AT THE FOLIES-BERGÈRES

Édouard Manet
1882
Courtauld Institute of Art Gallery, London
The Art Archive / DeA Picture Library

There's a spot-the-difference game to be played with the mirror image in this famous painting. Can you see what the painter has missed from the foreground?

A B C D E F G H I J K L M N O P Q R S T U V W X Y Z

A B C D E F G H I J K L M N O P Q R S T U V W X Y Z

**SAINT GEORGE
AND THE DRAGON**

Paolo Uccello
c. 1470
National Gallery, London
*The Art Archive / DeA Picture
Library / M. Carrieri*

Paolo Uccello was one of
the early pioneers of visual
perspective in art. In this
dramatic painting in the Late
Gothic style, the gathering
storm clouds behind Saint
George show that divine
intervention is at work.

ALLEGORICAL STILL LIFE

Balthasar van der Ast
1590–1656
Musée de la Chartreuse, Douai
The Art Archive /
DeA Picture Library

Butterflies were common in still-lives of the period as a symbol of resurrection; the apples are starting to spoil, a reminder of the ephemeral nature of human pleasures. Note the beautiful shells – within the still-life genre, shell painting was the artist's speciality.

A B C D E F G H I J K L M N O P Q R S T U V W X Y Z
1 2 3 4 5 6 7 8 9 10 11 12 13 14 15 16 17 18 19 20 21 22 23 24 25 26

INTERIOR WITH A YOUNG MAN HOLDING A RECORDER

Francesco Buoneri, known as Cecco di Caravaggio
c. 1610–1621
Ashmolean Museum, Oxford
The Art Archive / Ashmolean Museum

As his name suggests, the artist was a follower of Caravaggio, and was perhaps one of his models as a boy. Note the abundant variety of still-life objects pictured in this slightly enigmatic painting, including a wedge of cheese and a pie.

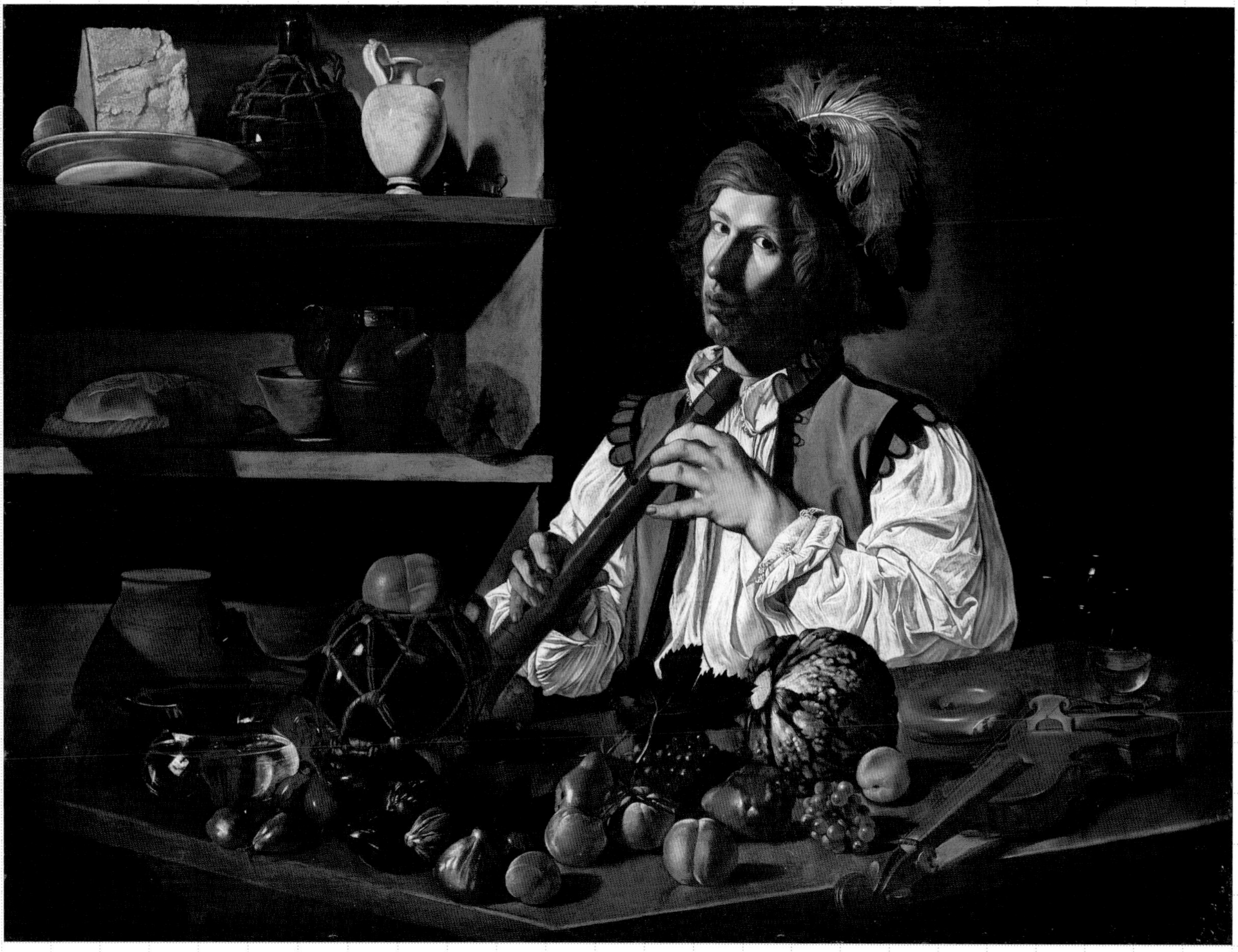

CHILDREN'S GAMES (DETAIL)

Pieter Bruegel the Elder
1560
Kunsthistorisches Museum, Vienna
The Art Archive / Kunsthistorisches Museum Vienna / Mondadori Portfolio/Electa

While it appears entirely light-hearted, this work makes a serious point, highlighting mankind's foolish preoccupation with their trivial earthly pursuits. Up to 80 different children's games have been identified within the painting; notice the two girls playing jacks with knucklebones at the bottom left.

A B C D E F G H I J K L M N O P Q R S T U V W X Y Z
1 2 3 4 5 6 7 8 9 10 11 12 13 14 15 16 17 18 19 20 21 22 23 24 25 26

**FANTASY INTERIOR
WITH THE FAMILY
OF JAN VAN GOYEN**

Jan Steen
c. 1661–1663
Nelson-Atkins Museum of Art,
Kansas City
*The Art Archive / Nelson-Atkins
Museum of Art / Superstock*

Although this is a fantasy
interior, there are numerous
details of seventeenth-century
Dutch life within the painting.
Notice the servant preparing
a platter of food through the
doorway and the brazier on the
floor. Can you see an elephant?

A B C D E F G H I J K L M N O P Q R S T U V W X Y Z

1 2 3 4 5 6 7 8 9 10 11 12 13 14 15 16 17 18 19 20 21 22 23 24 25 26

A B C D E F G H I J K L M N O P Q R S T U V W X Y Z

CHAIRING THE MEMBER

William Hogarth
1754–1755
Sir John Soane's Museum,
London
The Art Archive /
Sir John Soane's Museum /
Eileen Tweedy

In his depiction of the election of
an Oxfordshire MP, Hogarth is heavily
critical of the corruption rife in politics
and society at the time. Can you see
what the two chimney sweeps, sitting
on the wall to the right, are doing to
the unfortunate bear?

A B C D E F G H I J K L M N O P Q R S T U V W X Y Z

1 2

3 4 5 6 7 8 9 10 11 12 13 14 15 16 17 18 19 20 21 22 23 24 25 26

A B C D E F G H I J K L M N O P Q R S T U V W X Y Z

**THE MARCH OF THE GUARDS
TOWARDS SCOTLAND, 1745,
OR THE MARCH TO FINCHLEY**

**William Hogarth, colored
engraving by Luke Sullivan**
1750, published 1761
National Army Museum, London
*The Art Archive / National Army
Museum London*

The sign on the left, "Totenham Court
Nursery," shows the location of this
fictional mustering of troops. The cats
on the roof give a clue that the house
to the right is a "cattery" (brothel). Did
you see King Charles II's head on the
pub sign?

A B C D E F G H I J K L M N O P Q R S T U V W X Y Z

1 2 3 4 5 6 7 8 9 10 11 12 13 14 15 16 17 18 19 20 21 22 23 24 25 26

A B C D E F G H I J K L M N O P Q R S T U V W X Y Z

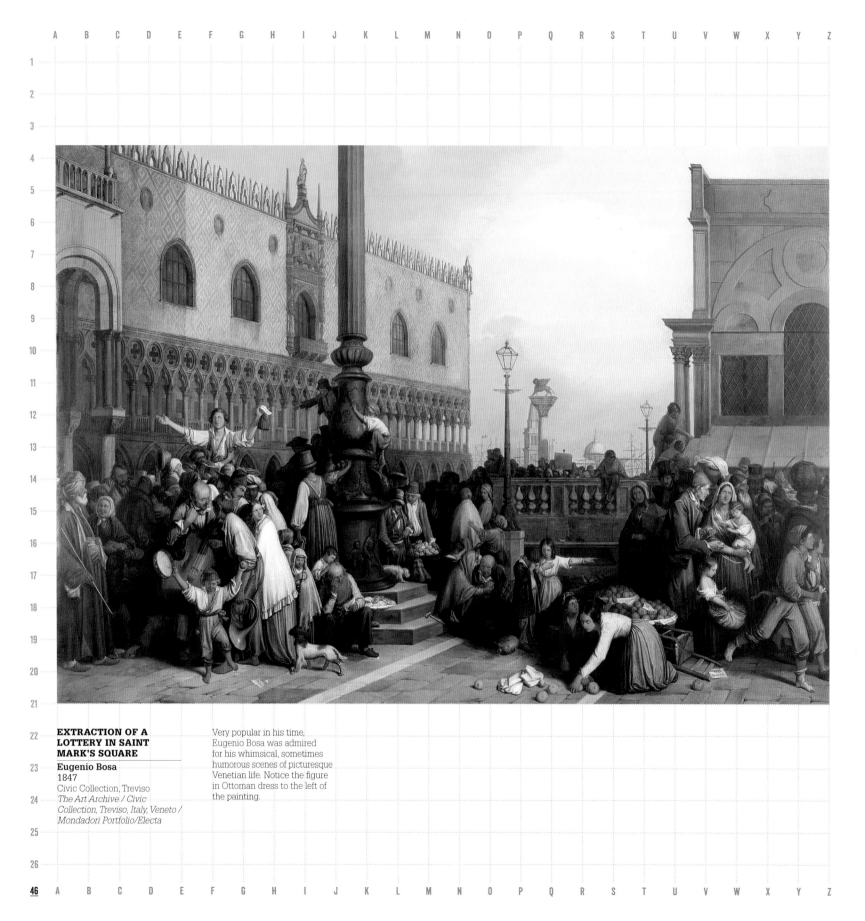

EXTRACTION OF A LOTTERY IN SAINT MARK'S SQUARE

Eugenio Bosa
1847
Civic Collection, Treviso
The Art Archive / Civic Collection, Treviso, Italy, Veneto / Mondadori Portfolio/Electa

Very popular in his time, Eugenio Bosa was admired for his whimsical, sometimes humorous scenes of picturesque Venetian life. Notice the figure in Ottoman dress to the left of the painting.

A B C D E F G H I J K L M N O P Q R S T U V W X Y Z

1
2
3
4
5
6
7
8
9
10
11
12
13
14
15
16
17
18
19
20
21
22
23
24
25
26

A B C D E F G H I J K L M N O P Q R S T U V W X Y Z

THE LUNCHEON

Claude Monet
1872–1876
Musée d'Orsay, Paris
*The Art Archive / Musée du
Louvre Paris / Superstock
to / Mondadori Portfolio/Electa*

In this painting depicting simple
family life – the remains of an
outdoor summertime lunch at
Monet's house at Argenteuil –
we can see Monet's wife Camille
strolling in the background and
their small son, Jean, playing to
the left of the table.

BULLFIGHT IN ST. MARK'S SQUARE, VENICE, ITALY

Giovanni Antonio Canaletto and Giovanni Battista Cimaroli
1697–1768 / 1687–1714
Biblioteca Estense, Modena
The Art Archive / Biblioteca Estense Modena / Collection Dagli Orti

Like many of the period, this painting records the pageantry and traditions of Venetian life. Here we can see the crowd mingling in the square with the bullfighters; there are spectators watching from all around, even from the façade of the Basilica.

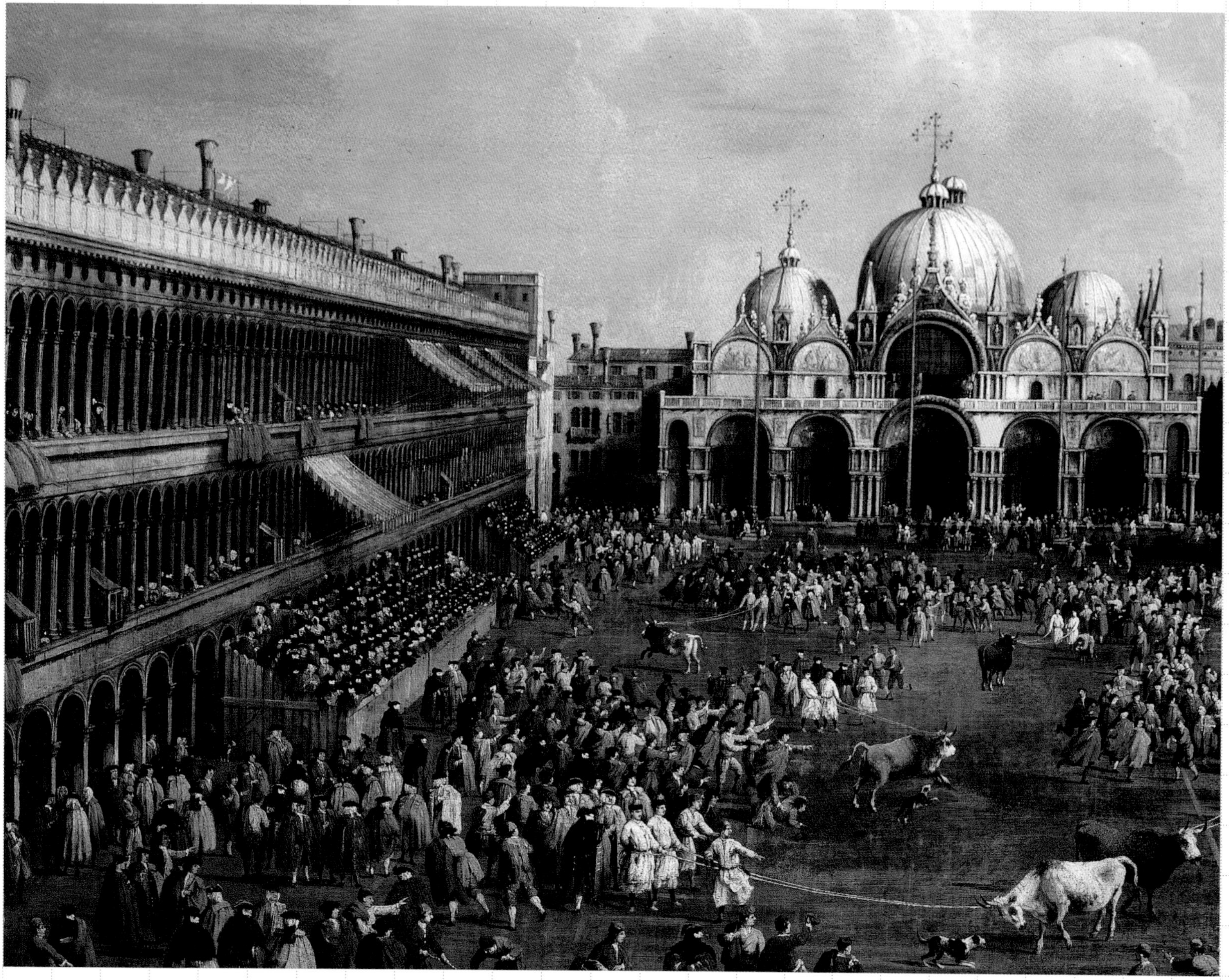

THE TEMPEST

Giorgio Giorgione
1506–1508
Gallerie dell'Accademia, Venice
The Art Archive / Accademia
Venice / Collection Dagli Orti

This enigmatic painting
continues to perplex art
historians. Are the broken
pillar and the white stork
heraldic emblems? Do the
man's two-toned stockings
have a meaning? And why
are the man and woman
so unperturbed by the
oncoming storm?

A B C D E F G H I J K L M N O P Q R S T U V W X Y Z

1 2 3 4 5 6 7 8 9 10 11 12 13 14 15 16 17 18 19 20 21 22 23 24 25 26

A B C D E F G H I J K L M N O P Q R S T U V W X Y Z

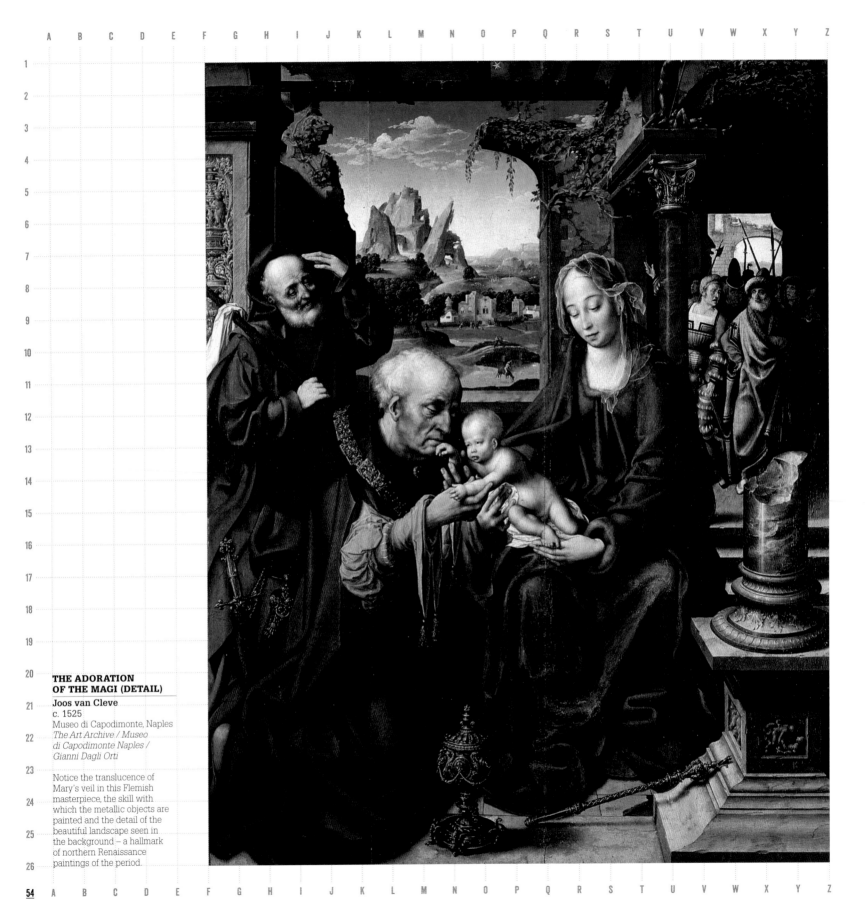

**THE ADORATION
OF THE MAGI (DETAIL)**

Joos van Cleve
c. 1525
Museo di Capodimonte, Naples
*The Art Archive / Museo
di Capodimonte Naples /
Gianni Dagli Orti*

Notice the translucence of
Mary's veil in this Flemish
masterpiece, the skill with
which the metallic objects are
painted and the detail of the
beautiful landscape seen in
the background – a hallmark
of northern Renaissance
paintings of the period.

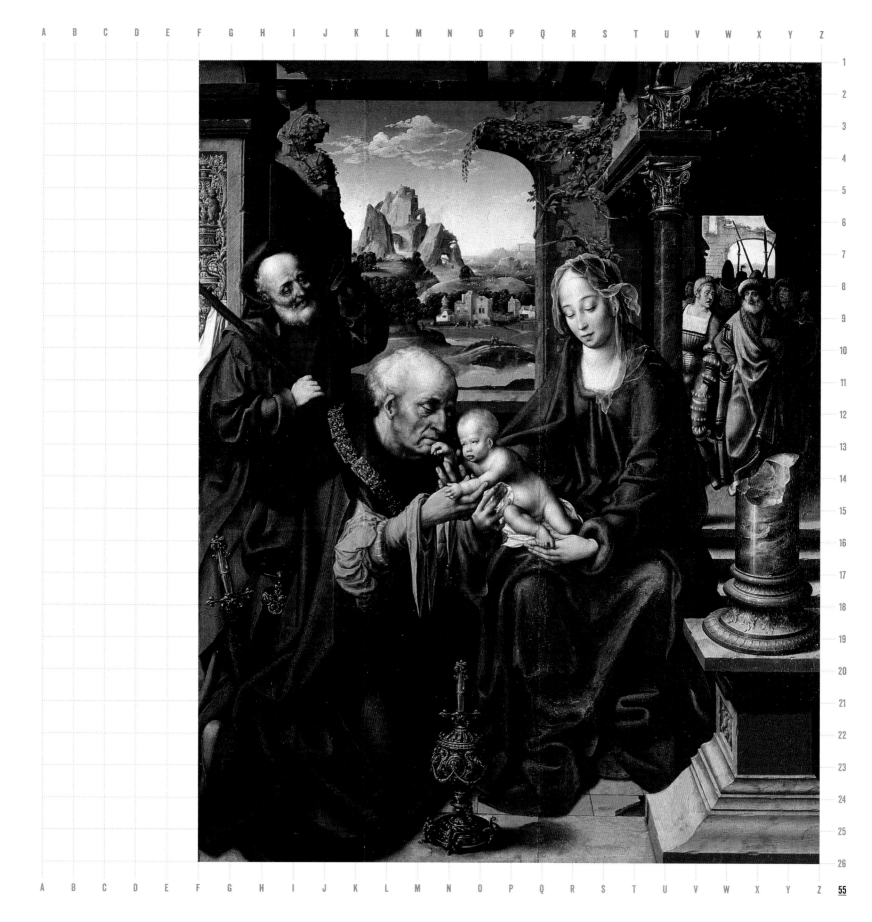

**THE RAFT OF
THE MEDUSA**

Théodore Géricault
1818–1819
Musée du Louvre, Paris
*The Art Archive /
Musée du Louvre Paris /
Gianni Dagli Orti*

The shipwreck of the Medusa in
1816 caused a massive political
scandal in France. Out of 150
people who drifted for days
on the makeshift raft, only ten
survived; we can see, far off in
the distance, the rescue ship
that failed in its mission.

A B C D E F G H I J K L M N O P Q R S T U V W X Y Z

1 2 3

4 5 6 7 8 9 10 11 12 13 14 15 16 17 18 19 20 21

22 23 24 25 26

A B C D E F G H I J K L M N O P Q R S T U V W X Y Z

ADORATION OF THE MAGI (DETAIL)

Gentile da Fabriano (Gentile di Niccolò)
1423
Galleria degli Uffizi, Florence
The Art Archive / Galleria degli Uffizi Florence / Mondadori Portfolio/Electa

Within this lavish and highly decorative altarpiece we can see the painter's patron Palla Strozzi, who commissioned the work, wearing a red hat. Notice the costumes of the period, decorated with gold and real precious stones. Can you spot a leopard?

A B C D E F G H I J K L M N O P Q R S T U V W X Y Z

1
2
3
4

5
6
7
8
9
10
11
12
13
14
15
16
17
18
19
20
21
22
23
24
25
26

A B C D E F G H I J K L M N O P Q R S T U V W X Y Z

**MARTYRDOM OF
SAINT CATHERINE**

Jacopo Dal Ponte (Jacopo Bassano)
1544
Civic Collections, Bassano del Grappa
*The Art Archive / Civic Collections,
Bassano del Grappa, Veneto, Italy /
Mondadori Portfolio/Electa*

In this highly dramatic, rather
disturbing Mannerist painting,
we can see the saint kneeling
before a spiked Catherine wheel,
atop a tangle of men and horses.
Above, an angel brings a crown.

MADONNA OF THE ROSARY

Lorenzo Lotto
1539
The Art Archive / Mondadori Portfolio/Electa

In this painting, Saint Esuperanzio, patron saint of the Cingoli, offers a model of the town to Mary. Did you notice the cleaver in the head of Saint Peter of Verona (far right)? The angels, together with baby John the Baptist, are scattering rose petals.

**PERSEUS AND
ANDROMEDA**

Giorgio Vasari
1572
Palazzo Vecchio, Florence
*The Art Archive / Palazzo
Vecchio Florence / A. Dagli Orti*

Notice the dragon's body
being winched to the land
in the background to the left.
Its blood has been transformed
into coral. The severed head of
the Medusa rests at Andromeda's
feet, with the mirror Perseus
used to protect himself from
being turned to stone.

A B C D E F G H I J K L M N O P Q R S T U V W X Y Z

1 2 3 4 5 6 7 8 9 10 11 12 13 14 15 16 17 18 19 20 21 22 23 24 25 26

A B C D E F G H I J K L M N O P Q R S T U V W X Y Z

THE KISS

Gustav Klimt
c. 1908
Österreichisches Galerie
Belvedere, Vienna
The Art Archive /
Österreichisches Galerie, Vienna /
Mondadori Portfolio/Electa

Klimt was inspired to paint using gold leaf by the Byzantine mosaics he saw in Ravenna during a visit in 1903. It's possible that this iconic painting, reproduced widely all over the world, is a self-portrait of the artist with his lover.

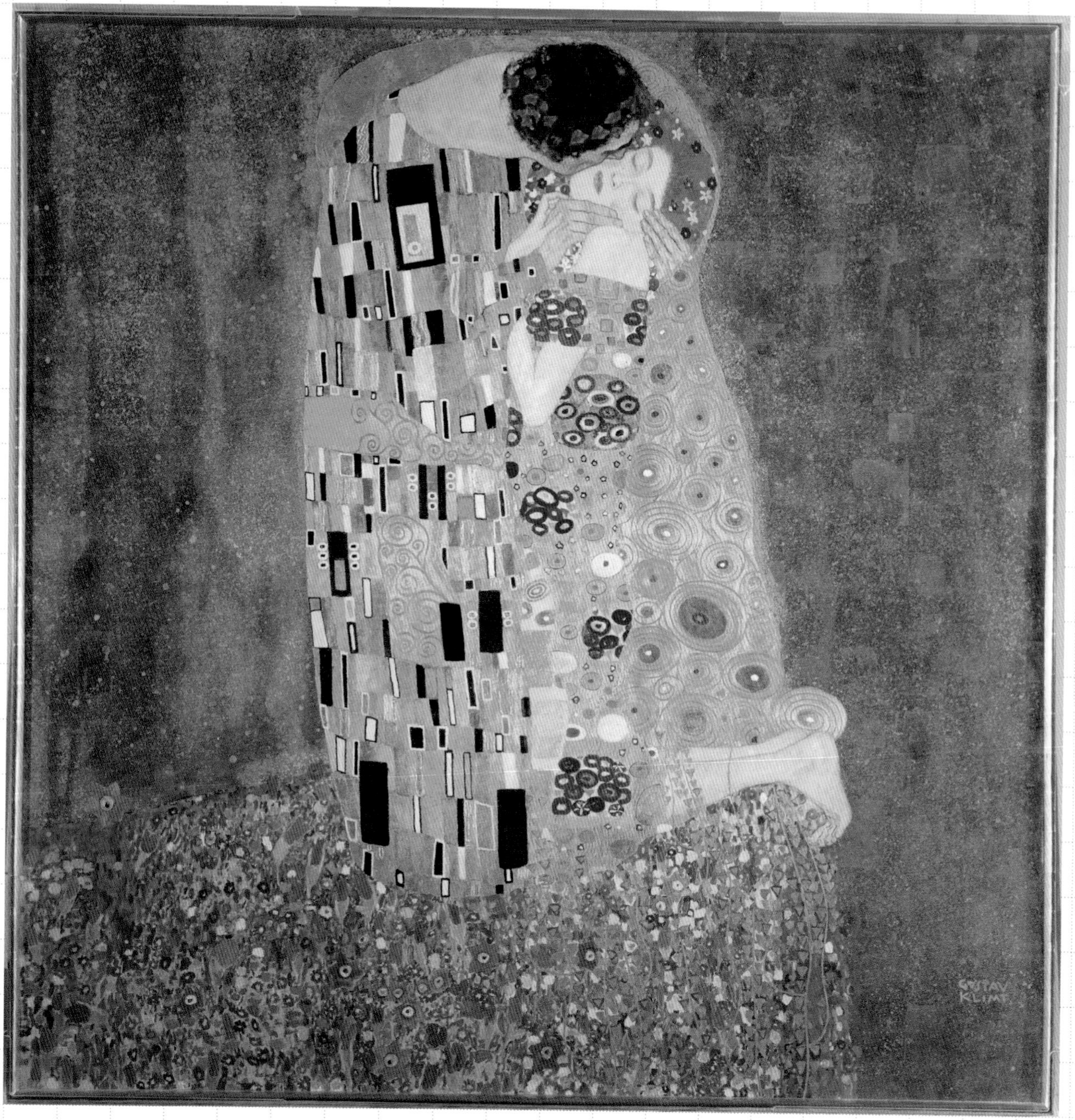

THE CROW IN PEACOCK FEATHERS

Frans Snyders
Date unknown
Pushkin Museum of Fine Arts, Moscow
The Art Archive / Pushkin Museum Moscow / Superstock

This painting depicts the sorry tale of the crow who struts in borrowed finery and is consequently humiliated. The ability to depict different textures, such as the feathers we can see here, was a particular skill of the artist.

A B C D E F G H I J K L M N O P Q R S T U V W X Y Z

1 2 3

4 5 6 7 8 9 10 11 12 13 14 15 16 17 18 19 20 21 22 23 24 25 26

A B C D E F G H I J K L M N O P Q R S T U V W X Y Z

TRIUMPH OF VIRTUE

Andrea Mantegna
c. 1502
Musée du Louvre, Paris
*The Art Archive / Musée du
Louvre Paris / Mondadori
Portfolio/Electa*

The figure on the left is
Minerva, chasing the Vices
from the Garden of Virtue.
Notice the centaur, the figure
with the monkey face, the flying
creatures with owl heads, and
the tree with a human form
to the left.

A B C D E F G H I J K L M N O P Q R S T U V W X Y Z

1 2 3 4 5 6 7 8 9 10 11 12 13 14 15 16 17 18 19 20 21 22 23 24 25 26

A B C D E F G H I J K L M N O P Q R S T U V W X Y Z

**ALTARPIECE OF SANTO SPIRITO
(ENTHRONED MADONNA WITH
ST. CATHERINE, ST. AUGUSTINE,
ST. SEBASTIAN, ST. ANTHONY THE
ABBOT, HOSTS OF ANGELS AND
ST. JOHN THE BAPTIST AS A CHILD)**

Lorenzo Lotto
1521
The Art Archive / Mondadori Portfolio/Electa

Notice the detailing on the
silk and on Saint Augustine's
robes, and the fine Turkish
carpet. Can you see the small
scroll with the painter's name
and date on it, sticking out from
beneath the fabric descending
from Mary's throne?

A B C D E F G H I J K L M N O P Q R S T U V W X Y Z

1 2 3 4 5 6 7 8 9 10 11 12 13 14 15 16 17 18 19 20 21 22 23 24 25 26

A B C D E F G H I J K L M N O P Q R S T U V W X Y Z

THE STAG HUNT OF THE ELECTOR FREDERICK THE WISE

Lucas Cranach the Elder
1529
Kunsthistorisches Museum, Vienna
The Art Archive / DeA Picture Library / G. Nimatallah

The Elector is the figure in the center; the other figures are probably Emperor Maximilian I and the painter's patron Elector Johann the Steadfast. Notice the beautifully observed buildings in the background, and the artist's insignia on the tree trunk.

A B C D E F G H I J K L M N O P Q R S T U V W X Y Z

1 2

21 22 23 24 25 26

A B C D E F G H I J K L M N O P Q R S T U V W X Y Z

THE AWAKENING CONSCIENCE

William Holman Hunt
1853
Tate Gallery, London
The Art Archive /
DeA Picture Library

This painting is of a lover and his mistress; note the absence of a wedding ring. Numerous symbols point to the idea of a sad and squandered life: the cat toying with a bird, the unfinished tapestry and the visible word "tears."

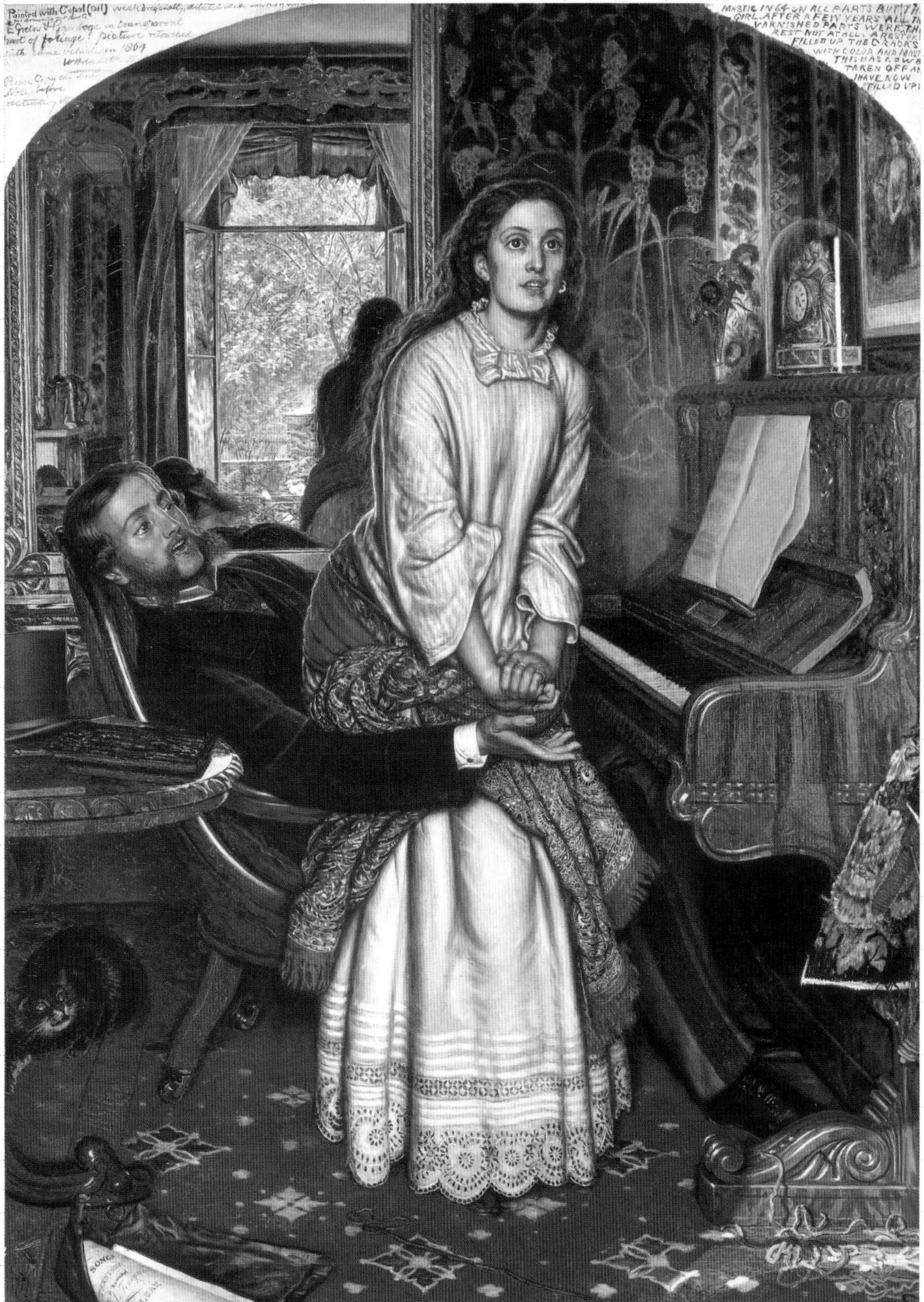

**MYSTIC MARRIAGE
OF SAINT CATHERINE**

Jan Brueghel the Elder
Date unknown
The Art Archive / Superstock

Carnations, tulips, snowdrops,
pansies and forget-me-nots
are among the flowers clearly
identifiable in the garland
surrounding the depiction of
the mystical marriage between
the infant Jesus and Saint
Catherine. Garland paintings
were a popular form of
devotional object in the
early seventeenth century.

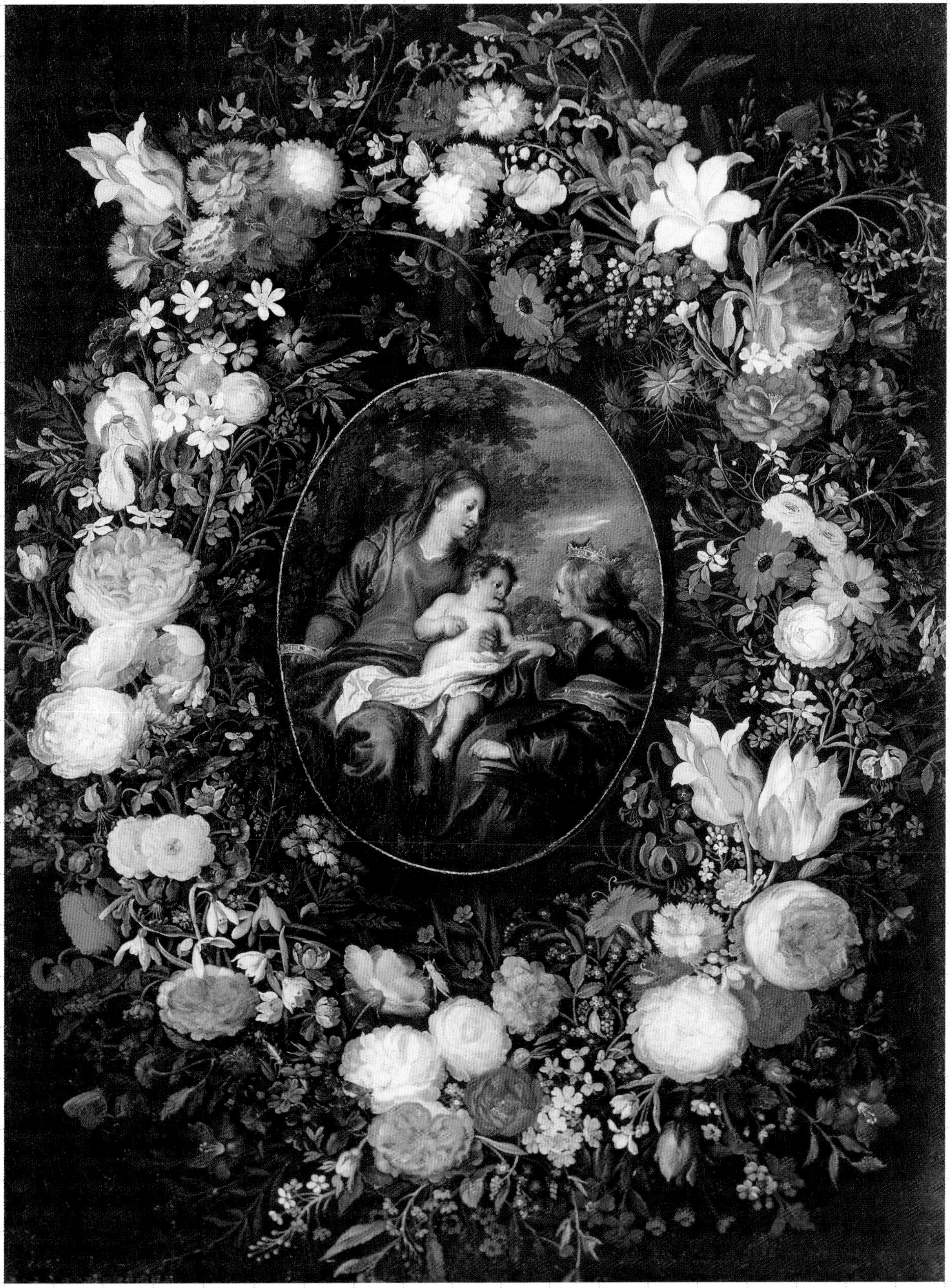

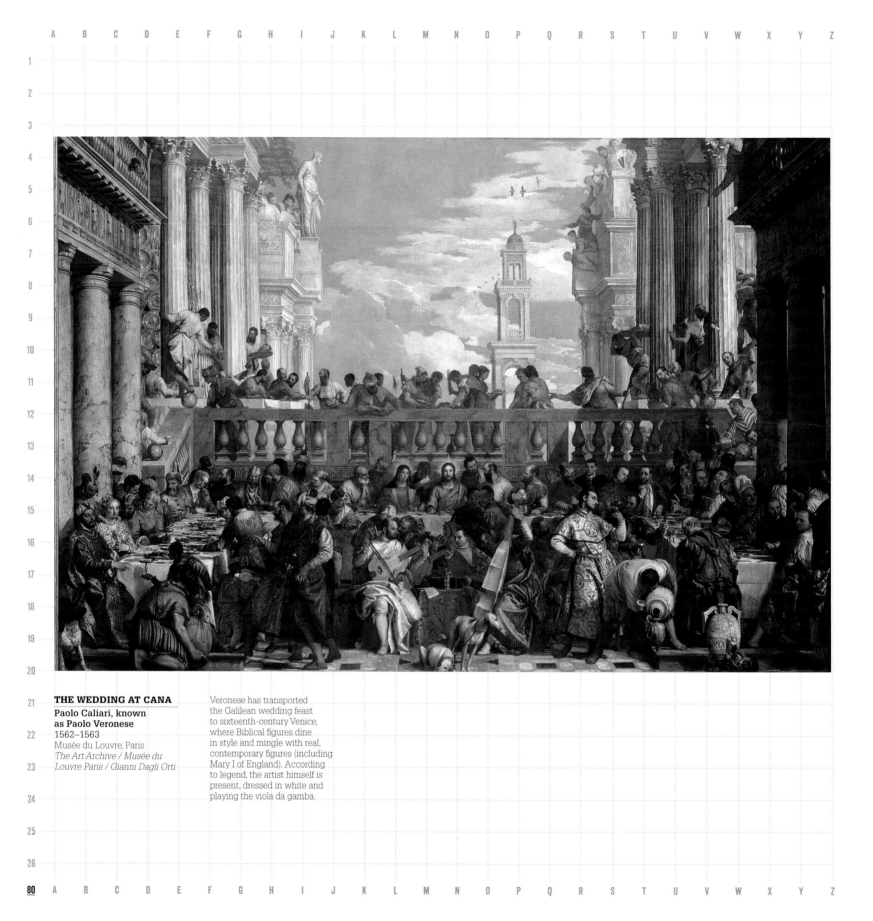

THE WEDDING AT CANA

**Paolo Caliari, known
as Paolo Veronese**
1562–1563
Musée du Louvre, Paris
*The Art Archive / Musée du
Louvre Paris / Gianni Dagli Orti*

Veronese has transported
the Galilean wedding feast
to sixteenth-century Venice,
where Biblical figures dine
in style and mingle with real,
contemporary figures (including
Mary I of England). According
to legend, the artist himself is
present, dressed in white and
playing the viola da gamba.

A B C D E F G H I J K L M N O P Q R S T U V W X Y Z

1 2 3 4 5 6 7 8 9 10 11 12 13 14 15 16 17 18 19 20 21 22 23 24 25 26

A B C D E F G H I J K L M N O P Q R S T U V W X Y Z

**THE GARDEN OF
EARTHLY DELIGHTS
(DETAIL)**

Hieronymus Bosch
c. 1500–1505
Museo del Prado, Madrid
*The Art Archive /
DeA Picture Library*

The central panel of this triptych
depicts the sinful world before
Noah's flood. The flowers and
the fruits may symbolize the
fleeting nature of the pleasures
of the flesh; the glass spheres
possibly represent the fragility
of human happiness. Looking
at the detail of the painting,
we can understand why
Hieronymus Bosch has been
called the first surrealist.

A B C D E F G H I J K L M N O P Q R S T U V W X Y Z

1 2 3 4 5 6 7 8 9 10 11 12 13 14 15 16 17 18 19 20 21 22 23 24 25 26

A B C D E F G H I J K L M N O P Q R S T U V W X Y Z

MADONNA AND CHILD ENTHRONED BETWEEN ANGELS AND SAINTS

Domenico Ghirlandaio
1486
Galleria degli Uffizi, Florence
The Art Archive / Galleria degli Uffizi Florence / Mondadori Portfolio/Electa

Within this ornate and colorful painting of Mary seated on her throne, notice the decorative illumination on the book held by Saint Thomas Aquinas to the right, the detailed gold decoration on the clothing, and the colored marble inlay on the wall behind the figures.

JULIUS CAESAR RECEIVING TRIBUTE OF EGYPT (DETAIL)

Andrea del Sarto and Alessandro Allori
1520
Villa Medicea, Poggio a Caiano
*The Art Archive /
DeA Picture Library / G. Roli*

The overall impression conveyed by this painting is one of abundance and exoticism. Notice the basket of shells, the pearl trim on the outfit of the figure to the left of the Emperor, and the elephant glimpsed in the background.

A B C D E F G H I J K L M N O P Q R S T U V W X Y Z

1
2

3 4 5 6 7 8 9 10 11 12 13 14 15 16 17 18 19 20 21 22 23 24 25 26

A B C D E F G H I J K L M N O P Q R S T U V W X Y Z

ANSWERS

P8
LA PRIMAVERA (SPRING) (DETAIL)
Giuseppe Arcimboldo

X2, Q13, J11, M21, S18, M7, Q16, O23, P3, R26, I12, J19, L14, P9, I3, N8, O24, S3, X9, G9

P10
LAS MENINAS (FAMILY OF KING PHILIP IV OF SPAIN) (DETAIL) / Diego Velázquez

J12, C8, I8, D6, P7, U15, Q8, R2, I3, E9, C20, I13, G10, R12, V18, M12, N7, Q7, C9, P10

P12
CHRIST IN THE HOUSE OF MARTHA AND MARY
Pieter Aertsen

Z8, U11, F7, C19, W5, N15, I6, P5, J13, P12, T9, B7, J7, R18, Q7, M13, G7, W16, W11, X6

P14
THE PARROT CAGE
Jan Steen

I3, O6, K25, I20, Y5, X23, Y17, S13, U13, I22, P2, I23, J24, M19, V11, G23, S18, K20, T7, V17

P16
THE COURTYARD OF A HOUSE IN DELFT
Pieter de Hooch

K7, L8, H10, G21, X10, R18, P19, K6, K3, N12, K11, J14, U11, G13, G18, T24, S8, X23, U9, V15

P18
A SUNDAY ON LA GRANDE JATTE
Georges Seurat

S9, E14, P9, W6, H12, K17, B5, J7, B12, F10, Q4, K10, N11, T8, W18, C7, Y10, Q13, R15, X20

P20
AMOROUS COUPLE
Johannes Vermeer

V15, L13, E12, E8, P9, R14, J10, V9, T16, W16, I8, Q16, U10, J3, N19, P10, D14, E17, G3, N6

P22
CHRIST PRESENTED TO THE PEOPLE
Quentin Massys

T4, P15, R6, V6, Q25, M22, H6, J3, J22, T17, N6, M4, J6, L9, X8, K18, U13, R1, T22, U22

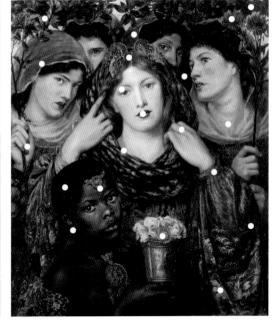

P24
THE BELOVED (THE BRIDE)
Dante Gabriel Rossetti

J16, P10, P5, S12, O13, O9, H7, I4, G13, O6, W3, M17, K20, R20, V11, Y2, V24, X19, S7, T16

P26
THE AMBASSADORS
Hans Holbein the Younger

S8, N21, Q16, Q5, M9, H13, T7, E8, H7, M16, R9, I10, M8, O10, O16, E21, 22U, P11, N15, L6, V22

P28
CABINET OF CURIOSITIES (WITH GLASS DOORS)
WITH VARIOUS OBJECTS
Andrea Domenico Remps

K10, J11, V6, L8, L19, D14, L12, J16, N8, O20, I16, W7, G16, V15, J18, J8, N13, W18, D18, D6

P30
A BAR AT THE FOLIES-BERGÈRES
Edouard Manet

M7, I15, M13, S15, W16, C4, H11, B3, O15, B18, H17, X3, M3, X19, N6, O11, M9, Y13, G19, X20

P32
SAINT GEORGE AND THE DRAGON
Paolo Uccello

K19, U12, L12, U13, E19, H10, L9, T2, W14, O13,
T11, E13, F15, H19, T8, P6, X10, P11, K17, V9

P34
ALLEGORICAL STILL LIFE
Balthasar van der Ast

X19, Q16, W17, N16, L13, E16, G5, J12, E13, O15,
S21, M17, T10, P19, O14, H21, R16, H16, M20, J17

P36
INTERIOR WITH A YOUNG MAN HOLDING A RECORDER
Francesco Buoneri, known as Cecco di Caravaggio

B5, V16, G10, N14, L17, S11, M13, I4, B16, M20, S18, O10, X18, J9,
W17, J16, I8, L10, D18, I14

P38
CHILDREN'S GAMES (DETAIL)
Pieter Bruegel the Elder

H13, K8, W3, K16, T24, Y25, N7, M9, H25, R12,
Y9, Y10, L19, O17, Q25, U6, T2, Y11, I16, G12

P40
**FANTASY INTERIOR WITH THE FAMILY
OF JAN VAN GOYEN** / Jan Steen

S7, L10, J18, H15, N7, Q9, P20, U20, X15, K14,
F16, U16, C19, O13, C12, C15, P19, K6, S18, X12

P42
CHAIRING THE MEMBER
William Hogarth

O6, D18, E10, N20, H18, U11, I12, O13, P16, N10,
Y15, V15, X10, L8, W6, D15, T13, T17, Q21, H7

P44
THE MARCH OF THE GUARDS TOWARDS SCOTLAND, 1745, OR THE MARCH TO FINCHLEY
William Hogarth / Luke Sullivan

K8, U5, R14, G18, M16, N14, Q10, Y11, Y7, B13, D10, J12, L10, L12, Q12, U22, K12, I17, S19, T13

P46
EXTRACTION OF A LOTTERY IN SAINT MARK'S SQUARE
Eugenio Bosa

U12, Q11, P10, O20, V20, K16, D20, I5, E4, D10, P11, Q15, S17, R13, Y14, M18, H12, L17, B17, Y7

P48
THE LUNCHEON
Claude Monet

M17, H12, C14, O2, V18, R18, P13, H6, P5, B10, R3, J14, N21, U7, D13, N15, S17, G14, K17, O18

P50
BULLFIGHT IN ST. MARK'S SQUARE, VENICE, ITALY
Giovanni Antonio Canaletto and Giovanni Battista Cimaroli

N8, W6, P15, W18, P9, K7, E14, R18, U10, G6, D10, T9, V16, Y19, X16, U4, N8, U15, I9, O8

P52
THE TEMPEST
Giorgio Giorgione

G16, O12, S8, Q5, I10, L10, X18, L14, R7, T12, Y7, P10, O18, S18, M8, G8, N10, V15, U7, J11

P54
THE ADORATION OF THE MAGI (DETAIL)
Joos van Cleve

X22, T8, W7, N6, M19, U24, O1, P11, H18, G9, V9, N21, L1, P4, M14, J7, W12, H19, U3, R7

P56
THE RAFT OF THE MEDUSA
Théodore Géricault

N8, P13, F8, E20, U9, R21, Q6, M9, C16, M19,
S14, X14, I16, U17, I18, X11, H5, O19, U19, K20

P58
ADORATION OF THE MAGI (DETAIL)
Gentile da Fabriano (Gentile di Niccolò)

K11, E7, T17, N6, Z11, Q5, Y8, W15, R18, D13,
U14, R7, D6, C9, M14, N10, O8, Q19, H11, K6

P60
MARTYRDOM OF SAINT CATHERINE
Jacopo Dal Ponte (Jacopo Bassano)

N9, P5, N3, V7, K9, L21, K12, K15, V20, L9, T18,
T7, H11, O15, Q17, V10, G10, K5, F18, N13

P62
MADONNA OF THE ROSARY
Lorenzo Lotto

V16, H17, I12, R3, R16, J15, N21, U22, G21, P24,
Q11, I5, L16, L20, R13, U18, J22, S15, N11, H13

P64
PERSEUS AND ANDROMEDA
Giorgio Vasari

X10, N8, T15, X2, I7, V13, V4, U11, M20, K20,
H17, R9, G8, I11, L8, L14, P21, Y7, J8, K7

P66
THE KISS
Gustav Klimt

K6, Q13, L13, L9, M4, S15, F17, S20, P6, J10, R16,
M13, O12, O15, N17, J20, J12, O4, Q5, Q6

P68
THE CROW IN PEACOCK FEATHERS
Frans Snyders

M6, R10, U20, Y5, U4, R4, R6, M10, Q10, X11,
B17, G16, M16, R15, V6, S19, L16, B10, M8, V8

P70
TRIUMPH OF VIRTUE
Andrea Mantegna

O13, O16, Y14, V12, V15, R15, L13, I3, P7, K20,
I18, M20, I12, P15, S12, B19, H16, T6, D20, X9

P72
ALTARPIECE OF SANTO SPIRITO (ENTHRONED MADONNA WITH ST. CATHERINE, ST. AUGUSTINE, ST. SEBASTIAN, ST. ANTHONY THE ABBOT, HOSTS OF ANGELS AND ST. JOHN THE BAPTIST AS A CHILD)** / Lorenzo Lotto

M21, O19, R12, U11, M3, H2, K4, J15, F21, M15, F6, V17,
U20, G11, H11, P15, W6, T5, M8, J11

P74
THE STAG HUNT OF THE ELECTOR FREDERICK THE WISE
Lucas Cranach the Elder

I8, J6, C4, D5, Z5, P10, E11, X4, X17, Y10, F9, B11, L18, N14, L13, K11, E14, C20,
P15, J9

P76
THE AWAKENING CONSCIENCE
William Holman Hunt

L5, Q25, R13, U10, I9, O6, P8, U7, R16, G14, V16,
V23, I26, O20, G22, V6, R5, X3, T25, M25

P78
MYSTIC MARRIAGE OF SAINT CATHERINE
Jan Brueghel the Elder

Q15, K14, K7, P20, H19, S25, R12, U16, I4, T7, T3, W23,
K19, V3, J23, L13, M25, H7, S19, P7

P80
THE WEDDING AT CANA
Paolo Caliari, known as Paolo Veronese

I5, P5, P6, R7, N11, L11, E12, D17, L17, O19, F10,
P13, J11, V9, S11, C14, K18, P20, V18, V16

P82
THE GARDEN OF EARTHLY DELIGHTS (DETAIL)
Hieronymus Bosch

L12, O13, T8, R8, R4, U4, V5, Y6, H5, S13, M20, N17,
I10, M8, Q6, Y4, G9, I11, K10, N12

P84
**MADONNA AND CHILD ENTHRONED
BETWEEN ANGELS AND SAINTS**
Domenico Ghirlandaio

S5, R2, S4, C5, V7, S11, E10, N18, M21, F3, J2,
C2, Q3, P5, Q21, G18, G5, F7, O11, V9

P86
**JULIUS CAESAR RECEIVING TRIBUTE
OF EGYPT (DETAIL)**
Andrea del Sarto and Alessandro Allori

F5, K4, B5, B15, O12, U4, T3, X9, E9, D18, S15,
S16, Z13, O14, K12, D3, S5, Z5, Y10, Z7